TIGERS
DON'T EAT
GRASS

TIGERS DON'T EAT GRASS

Ronald Jenkins

Oriental and Occidental
Aphorisms on the Life of Business
and the Business of Life

EBURY PRESS   LONDON

Published by Ebury Press
Division of The National Magazine
Company Ltd
Colquhoun House
27–37 Broadwick Street
London W1V 1FR

This book is dedicated to the
members of the Rotary club of
Surbiton who first suggested that I
should make these proverbs
available to a wider public.

British Library Cataloguing
in Publication Data
Jenkins, Ronald,
    Tigers don't eat grass:
    oriental and occidental
    aphorisms on the life of business
    and the business of life.
    1. Aphorisms, to 1988.
    Anthologies
    I. Title
    808.882

ISBN 0 85223 743 X

Editors Sarah Bailey and
Heather Rocklin
Art Director Frank Phillips
Designer Tony Paine
Illustrations Angela McAllister

Filmset by Advanced Filmsetters
(Glasgow) Ltd
Printed and bound in Great Britain
at The Bath Press, Avon

Contents

FOREWORD

It is frequently said in the West that 'Managers are born, not made', but I favour the oriental version which says, 'Of wisdom, half comes with birth, half with learning.'

When I first became a manager, I was sent to a famous business school, where I was to be taught the art of successful management. The school was a great disappointment; the lecturers were mostly academics who proved their theories with carefully chosen case-studies, and who believed that, on completion of the course, the managers would go out into a perfect business world, populated by reasonable, logical people who would all know the rules by which the business school games were played. My own experience suggested otherwise, but I thought it only fair to give it a try.

On leaving the school I was posted to the Far-East to manage a subsidiary company. Whenever a problem arose I would get out my course notes and textbook on the Doppler-Pego method of decision making, but by the time I had found a vaguely similar example and translated the jargon, the problem had often solved itself—and not always to the best advantage!

I began to notice that my Chinese colleagues did not agonize over problems as I did. Instead there was a brief discussion, a definitive statement, a nod of agreement by all those discussing the matter, and away they went to administer the solution. I began to consult them rather than my text books.

I had to relocate a very aggressive and abrasive young manager, who had been brilliantly successful in carrying out a difficult and harrowing task. Only two openings were available at the time: a quiet, safe job, or another tough assignment which carried promotion but had an uncertain outcome. The former would be no challenge for him, and as for the latter, it just didn't seem fair to plunge him back into battle so soon. I agonized over the problem and eventually spoke about it to the chief cashier, a wise old Chinese of many years service who knew everyone in the company. He pondered for a very short time, tapped my blotter with his pencil, said 'Tigers don't eat grass', and went about his business. End of problem! I offered the tough job to the young manager and he leapt at it!

Shortly after this, I was considering appointing joint managing directors in a newly merged subsidiary of the company. My Chinese banker friend laughed when I told him and said, 'When two men ride a horse one must ride behind.'

I soon realized that my oriental friends appeared to have something that was missing from my business school teaching: they had a complete philosophy for the people actually living through the daily rack of running a business. Sometimes we do not do as well as we might have done, or as well as others expect. Business language is not very good at letting us down lightly in such situations. We need something which sounds better than 'I goofed this time, but it wasn't all my fault, and I am not really an idiot. We need to be able to save face. My oriental friends were a rich source of such sayings and I began gathering proverbs, folk sayings, aphorisms, and epigrams, mainly of the Orient but also from other sources, and I tried using some of them.

My first opportunity arose after the chairman had sent a resolution to be put at an important trade conference. The resolution was overwhelmingly defeated. This was not good news for me to send and I felt the need to let him down lightly, so I concluded my message with, 'Even a silver trumpet may not prevail above a score of brazen horns.' He was tickled pink; it had saved his face.

Condolences are always difficult. On the death of a colleague, I wrote to his widow, 'His kindness was as deep as the sea, and his integrity as firm as a mountain.' This phrase was read at his memorial service, and his widow later told me that it had given her both solace and a feeling of pride.

I have often called upon my collection of sayings in my private as well as my business life. I have, for example, told my children that 'To understand why your parents love you, you must first have children of your own', and I have given them appropriate words of wisdom as various crises arose. I have learned that 'Small children, small problems. Big children, big problems', and this still holds true as they enter their thirties.

Now that I have retired from active business, and use my store of sayings for private occasions only, my friends have urged me to make them available to a wider public, and so I have gone into print. I shall not be downcast if the enterprise is not a great success, for 'Not every oyster contains a pearl', and if a few readers can find guidance or comfort in the following pages, I shall be content. At the very least, if you have got this far, I can leave you with an old Irish farewell: 'May the road rise up to meet you. May the wind be always at your back. May the sun shine warm upon your face and the rain fall soft upon your head; and, until we meet again, may God hold you in the palm of his hand.'

R. F. JENKINS

9

Accountants

The accountant is the man who goes on to the battlefield after the battle is over, to count the dead and bayonet the wounded.

The withered hand on the controls.

Advice

Repeat a piece of good advice three times, and even a dog will get bored.

Better ask ten times, than get lost once.

Ask advice wherever you will, but act according to your own judgement.

Anger

He who holds back rising anger like a rolling chariot, him I call a real driver.

Hungry men are angry men.

Anger in debate causes the argument to be forgotten.

Appearances

There is many a good man to be found under a shabby hat.

Not everyone at whom dogs bark is a thief.

Any man surrounded by dwarfs looks like a giant.

We know men's faces, not their minds.

A fly on the window may be taken for an eagle in the sky.

We always think that others are enjoying themselves.

Eat according to your means, but dress above them.

His face was filled with broken commandments.

Aspirations

A toad has to pass a very severe examination before it can become a dragon.

He who fails to become a giant need not remain content with being a dwarf.

Do not worry about not holding high positions; worry rather about playing your proper role.

Avarice

Avarice can never be satisfied.

If a man could turn stone into gold, still would his heart never be content.

Beauty

Beauty is a feast in itself.

She possesses a beauty which causes the fish to dive and the wild geese to settle on the ground, the moon to hide its face and the flowers to blush.

Beautiful women are often ill-fated.

When beauty declines, love ebbs.

Behaviour

One cry astonishes people.

He is skilled in human relations. Even after long acquaintance he is respectful towards others.

Fortune does not change men, it only unmasks them.

In a mad country, normal behaviour is an act of madness.

Make me good oh Lord—but not today!

They are as they are, because they like being as they are.

If you treat an individual as he is, he will stay as he is, but if you treat him as if he were what he ought to be and could be, he will behave as if he were what he ought to be and could be.

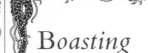

Bigotry

For the blind in mind there is no physician.

People see things in the way they want to see them. They judge people by themselves.

Black Sheep

Every family cooking pot has one black spot.

A rolling stone gathers no moss, but it does acquire a certain polish.

Boasting

They promise mountains and perform molehills.

People without talent boast of their ancestors.

A little coin in a large jar makes a great noise.

He who kills tigers does not wear rat-skin sleeves.

He who enters as a whirlwind will depart as an ant.

Bores and Boredom

A bore is a person who drills a hole in one's spirit.

When a bore leaves the room you feel as if someone just came in.

A bore is someone who insists on talking about himself, instead of listening to you talking about yourself.

I spent a year in that town, one Sunday.

Bureaucrats

The friendship of officials is as thin as paper.

Flee the devil, but stay with him if the alternative is a government official.

An official never flogs a bearer of gifts.

Officials mutually protect themselves.

A bureaucrat treats human life like weeds and straw.

In the modern state more time is often spent in running bureaucracies than in defining their purpose.

Capitalism

The misery of being exploited by capitalists is nothing to the misery of not being exploited.

The meek shall inherit the earth, but not the mineral rights.

Economic ideas that are admirable in their supporting theory can prove sadly deficient in practice.

Character

Ivory does not grow in the mouth of a dog.

Distance tests a horse's strength; time reveals a man's character.

The salt can never be quite washed out of sea-water.

Authority usually stems from character.

Snails and bulls both have horns, but their natures are not similar.

Even though a snake enters a bamboo tube, it is still inclined to wriggle.

Charity

If thou art forced to beg, knock on the door of the rich.

A good deed has many claimants.

Good deeds are full of vicissitudes.

If you do not ask their help, all men are good-natured.

Children

Children's children are the crown of old men.

To understand why your parents love you, you must raise children of your own.

When a son has grown up he lives in his own world.

A father loves his children, but they love their children.

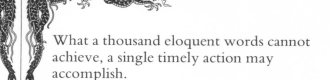

To give a son a thousand pieces of gold is not equal to teaching him one craft.

Do not confine your children to your own learning, for they were born in another time.

Other people's harvests are always the best harvests, but one's own children are always the best children.

Common Sense

Prescribe the medicine according to the ailment.

Common sense is not so common!

What a thousand eloquent words cannot achieve, a single timely action may accomplish.

Complaints

Treat complaints as carefully as one would treat a sore.

People remember how you dealt with a complaint, long after they have forgotten what the complaint was about.

Confidence

The man who has confidence in himself gains the confidence of others.

If water is too clear it will contain no fish; men who are too cautious will never gain wisdom.

Confidence is that quiet, assured feeling, just before you fall on your face.

Conscience

If all your life you have a clear conscience, you need not fear a knock on the door at midnight.

Never fail to suspect yourself when you find that you are getting up a great army of reasons to prove that what you are about to do is right.

Contentment

God wants us to be rich and comfortable.

To pursue happiness is to flee from contentment.

He who is content is wealthy.

Man's nature asks no more than that, free from bodily pain, he may exercise his mind agreeably, free from fear and anxiety.

A man that loves his own fireside, and can govern his house without falling by the ears with his neighbour, or engaging in suits of law, is as free as a duke of Venice.

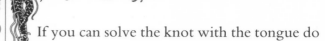

It breaks no law to be comfortable.

One joy dispels a hundred cares.

Controversy

Quarrel is the weapon of the weak.

There is a time to silence an adversary with the honey of logical persuasion, and there is a time to silence him with the argument of a heavily directed club.

In three moments a labourer will move an obstructing rock, but three moons will pass without two wise men agreeing on the meaning of a vowel.

If you can solve the knot with the tongue do not solve it with the teeth.

A man never tells you anything till you contradict him.

Correction

To dig up a tree, you must begin with the root.

The mortar must harden if the wall is to hold good.

What is directed equally against all can single out no one.

Corruption

A dry finger cannot take up salt.

Thou shalt not muzzle the ox when he treads out the corn.

You can't get fat from a dry bone.

When the upper beams are not straight, the lower ones will be crooked also.

How much swifter is the progress of corruption than its cure.

The corruption of the people originates in the corruption of the leaders.

You cannot buy a politician—you can only rent him.

Courage

There will always be a brave man to respond to a high reward.

Cowards die many times before their deaths; the valiant never taste of death but once.

You would be surprised by how often nerve succeeds.

Sometimes it needs more courage to decline to jump a fence in the face of a large field, than to go for it and break your neck.

Men of principle have courage.

Crime

The culprit often makes the first accusation.

Prevention of crime depends not on the severity but on the certainty of punishment.

There is violence in human nature. There are only three ways of trying to deal with it: persuasion, prevention, or punishment.

Criticism

It is much easier to be critical than correct.

If you don't joke at my fat nose, I won't laugh at your bald head.

Clean your finger before you point at my spots.

Those who have free seats at the play, hiss first.

Good medicine is bitter in the mouth.

The tongue is like a sharp knife; it kills without drawing blood.

Assassination is the most extreme form of censorship.

A yawn is a silent shout.

Culture

Within the four walls of the arts, all men are brothers.

Music first and last should sound well, should allure and enchant the ear—never mind the inner significance.

Intellectual food is like any other; it is more pleasant and more beneficial to take it with a spoon than with a shovel.

The average Englishman is not in passionate need of the arts, and opera least of all.

Muzak Chewing gum for the ears.

She invariably was first over the fence in the mad pursuit of culture.

Cunning

The mighty dragon is no match for the native serpent.

Where the lion's skin will not reach, you must patch it out with fox fur.

The local snake.

A tiger's head but a serpent's tail.

Custom

Every custom begins as a broken precedent.

Relinquish an evil custom even though it be of thy fathers and ancestors; adopt a good custom even though it be established among thine enemies.

Danger

The tiger that has once tasted blood is dangerous.

There is meat at one end of a boar but sharp tusks at the other.

It is difficult to get off the back of a tiger.

A blind man riding a blind horse approaching a deep gorge at midnight.

In peril, risking one's life is probably the only way to survive.

The fuller the cup, the sooner the spill.

Death

To study philosophy, is to learn to die.

When the oil is exhausted, the lamp goes out.

To travel to the kingdom of the immortals.

We should always, as near as we can, be booted and spurred, ready to go.

If the rich could hire the poor to die for them, the poor would make a very good living.

Nature has ordered only one door into life, but a hundred thousand ways out.

To be born is in the course of nature, but to die is according to the decree of destiny.

One cannot live forever by ignoring the price of coffins.

Decisions

Every road leads in two directions.

The choice of Achilles: a short life full of deeds, or a long one full of regrets.

The man who does not make a choice, makes a choice.

Talk is only a means to an end; discussion must be turned into decision, and decision into action.

A wise man makes his own decisions; an ignorant man follows public opinion.

When you have no choice, at least be brave.

He who considers everything, decides nothing.

Despair

There is no vulture like despair.

A drowning man will grab even the point of a sword.

Even a trapped beast struggles.

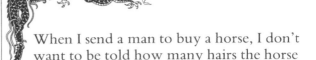

He who has nothing to lose can try anything.

The worst is not always the most certain.

The cornered rat bites the cat.

Details

Triviality To count rice grains for cooking.

Once one occupies oneself with the big, one loses interest in the small.

He is the kind of man who wonders whether a flea has a navel.

When I send a man to buy a horse, I don't want to be told how many hairs the horse has in its tail. I wish only to know its points.

Diligence

Running water does not get stale.

See thou a man diligent in his ways, he shall stand before kings.

Better return home and make a net, than long for fish on the edge of the pond.

Everyone with a body has two servants—his hands and his feet.

Practice is the fruit of theory.

The hinge of a door is never crowded with insects.

Never say 'it cannot be done'. Always say 'I do not know if it can be done, but I will try'.

Discretion

When with dwarfs do not talk about pygmies.

The dog that would retain his bone, shuns observation.

He who proves too much proves nothing.

A teaspoon of honey will trap more flies than a quart of vinegar.

Don't tie your shoes in a melon field, nor adjust your hat under a fig tree.

When it is enough, stop.

Among roses, be a rose; among thorns, be a thorn.

Questions are never indiscreet but answers sometimes are.

Dishonesty

He who steals an egg will steal a camel.

A guilty man runs when no one is chasing him.

He is giving a crumbling house a whitewash.

It is not hard to deceive people—*once*.

He says he abhors dampness yet he lives in a low place.

Get your facts first and then you can distort them as much as you please.

All thieving depends upon a receiver.

Of a stolen item It has flown away without the aid of wings.

Divided Responsibility

If two men ride on horseback, one must ride behind.

When two persons are in charge of a horse, it is bound to get thin.

One mountain cannot harbour two tigers.

Heaven does not have two suns.

D.I.Y. *and Hobbies*

Before you do anything, something else must first be done.

Working slowly will produce fine goods.

Do not waste days in idleness—the bright spring will not come this way again.

Black holes exist in space, and in workshop floors. Screws and nuts fall into them and are never seen again.

When a habit begins to cost money, it is called a hobby.

Doctors

A wise doctor never treats himself.

We live off only a quarter of what we swallow. Doctors live off the other three quarters.

Drinking

Buddha taught that a man who takes liquor and forces another to drink will be reborn five hundred times without hands.

An innkeeper never worries if your appetite is big.

Economics

Nothing is for nothing, even if the pasha were thy brother.

Monetary policy is like a string: you can pull it through with incalculable results, but you cannot shove it at all.

People who talk about gradually inflating might as well talk about firing a gun off gradually.

Emergencies

An emergency is a situation in which immediate and drastic action is needed to forestall disaster.

When one is inquiring for a way of escape from an advancing tiger, flowers of speech assume the form of noisome bindweed.

Employment

Changing jobs To jump to another trough.

Dismissal To break a man's rice-bowl.

Enemies

If you strike a snake without killing it, it will turn and bite you.

You should always forgive your enemies, for nothing annoys them more.

Though you bind a fallen enemy hand and foot, yet can he still follow you with curses.

Dragon encircling, tiger crouching.

It is good luck for a man if his enemy is wise.

Evil

It is easier to contend with evil at the first than at the last.

Hide the evil, show the good.

Excellence

Genius does what it must, and talent what it can.

Great skill looks like the lack of it.

Excellence does not remain alone. It is sure to attract neighbours.

Respect the man who is a little better than his word, a little more liberal than his promise, a little larger in deed than he is in speech.

Excess

Too far East is West.

Even dragons know better than to appear too often.

The expense of the pursuit sometimes exceeds the value of the prize.

To exceed is not necessarily to excel.

He uses a cannon to shoot a sparrow.

The archer that shoots over, misses as much as he that falls short.

Excuses

Those who want to beat a dog, always find a stick.

Ten excuses are less persuasive than one.

His excuse is graver than his injury.

Experience

The old horse knows the way.

The learning for which you pay will be remembered longer.

By much falling, the child learns to walk.

If you wish to know the road ahead, inquire of those who have travelled it.

Adversity makes a man wise—but not rich.

'I heard' is not as good as 'I saw'.

Inexperience He has a smell of wet milk.

Experts

Even when the experts all agree, they may well be mistaken.

Even a mole may instruct a philosopher in the art of digging.

The progress of science is strewn, like an ancient desert trail, with the bleached skeletons of discarded theories which once seemed to possess eternal life.

Those who cannot sing, can still be experts on singing.

Failure

Those intending to walk a hundred miles, often stop at ninety.

Not every oyster holds a pearl; not every time does the archer hit the target.

He who has failed three times, sets up as an instructor.

The man who has not tasted the bitter does not know what the sweet is.

Not everyone who comes down your street enters by your door.

Even a silver trumpet may not prevail above a score of brazen horns.

Some of the roads must lead nowhere.

Familiarity

Living near the temple, one loses respect for the gods.

The first time it is a favour; the second, a rule.

Water is the most indifferent thing so long as we have it, the most precious as soon as we want it.

Fanaticism

Fanaticism consists of a redoubling of your efforts when you have forgotten your aim.

He has spear lips and a sword tongue.

Fate

When we talk of tomorrow, the gods laugh.

Fortune is a wheel that turns with great speed.

Heaven's web and earth's net.

Men do not seek tragedy but it lies in wait for them when they least expect it.

Water once poured out will flow as freely to the north as to the south.

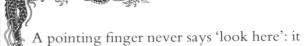

The hands of the gods are slow to close, but their arms are extremely long.

Man has a thousand schemes, heaven has but one.

Although destiny is blind, it can see through a marble wall. Immovable, it will outstrip the swiftest horse, and however often a man may turn in order to avoid pursuit, he will in the end walk unheedingly into what has been arranged for his reception.

Faults

He who seeks for a faultless brother, will remain brotherless.

A pointing finger never says 'look here': it says 'look there'.

The hunchback does not see his own hump.

I have yet to meet a man who, on observing his own faults, blamed himself.

He knows that others would throw him down, and therefore he had better lie down softly of his own accord.

Fighters

If his legs fail him, he fights on his knees.

When the shield is bent the sword is also blunted.

Flexibility

The wisdom of concession.

Where four can stand at all, five can just squeeze.

When the wind is great, bow before it; when the rain is heavy, yield to it.

During a violent storm, the reed that bends survives; the oak that resists, perishes.

One who can both stoop and stand erect.

If you cannot do what you want, do what you can.

Folly

An old cat burning his whiskers.

The wiser the sage, the more profound the folly.

Provoking the powerful To catch lice on the tiger's head.

A good folly is worth whatever you pay for it.

There is no economy in going to bed early to save candles, if the result be twins.

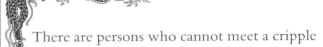

The beggar who wears a costly silk robe, displays his sores in vain.

If you are going to do something wrong, at least enjoy it.

Food

Whatever satisfies hunger is good food.

God sends meat and the Devil sends cooks.

Fools

Every village has its idiot.

There are persons who cannot meet a cripple without talking about feet.

There are well dressed foolish ideas, just as there are well dressed fools.

It is impossible to make anything foolproof, because fools are so ingenious.

Let us be thankful for the fools; but for them the rest of us could not succeed.

If he had twice as much sense he would be an idiot.

The world always contains one more fool than you think.

A fool and his money are soon married.

Forgiving

The perfection of forgiveness is to not mention the offence.

The past should be forgiven, even though it cannot be forgotten.

Friends

In prosperity our friends know us. In adversity, we know our friends.

The visit of a friend is medicine to the sick.

What is offered in friendship should not be weighed upon a scale.

Who asks more of a friend than he can bestow, deserves to be refused.

A friendship founded on business is better than a business founded on friendship.

A friendly smile is a key to security and a lamp to benevolence.

What was begun in friendship should not be wound up in malice.

Wine and meat friends.

The Future

The falling of a single leaf will remind us of autumn.

The one thing that is predictable, is the unseen.

The future isn't what it used to be.

One generation plants the trees under whose cool shade another generation rests.

It is wise to look ahead, but foolish to look further than you can see.

Gambling

He who believes in gambling will live to sell his sandals.

The urge to gamble is so universal, and its practice so pleasurable, that I assume it must be evil.

Good News

As cold water to a thirsty soul, so is good news from a far country.

Good news fattens the bones.

Good Wishes

Your kindness is as deep as the sea, your integrity is as firm as a mountain.

Clear rivers and calm seas.

May your age be as old as a mountain and your happiness as deep as the sea.

May the road rise up to meet you. May the wind be always at your back. May the sun shine warm upon your face and the rain fall safe upon your head, and until we meet again may God hold you in the palm of his hand.

Happiness

It's pretty hard to tell what does bring happiness; poverty and wealth have both failed.

'Are you unhappy?'
'No.'
'Then you must be happy. Do not confuse rare moments of ecstasy with happiness.'

Hatred

Hatred blinds you to others' virtues.

Hatred which enters the bones and marrow.

Heat and Cold

Heat belongs to all, cold varies with the clothing.

After the intense cold comes the spring.

Honesty

An honest magistrate has lean clerks; a powerful god has fat priests.

All roads to wealth are easy if you do not mind the mud.

It is annoying to be honest to no purpose.

In the game of life, it is better to score by honours than by tricks.

Hope

Hope is a good breakfast, but a bad supper.

Even a mole can turn its eyes upwards.

Disperse the clouds and mists, and there is the blue sky.

To the desert traveller, all wells are sparkling.

Through dark willow trees to bright flowers.

Husbands

Never trust a husband too far or a bachelor too near.

Husbands can forget anything—except when to eat.

Men should take care not to make women weep, for God counts their tears.

Ignorance

Do not assume that an ignorant man is a stupid man.

He who has seen little, marvels much.

Like stepping on a tiger's tail.

Illness

To the suffering, a day passes like a year.

'I wasn't feeling well.' I think in time you may perhaps find that most of the work in this world is done by people who aren't feeling well.

Illusory

Only flowers in a mirror.

Autumn wind passing by the ear.

Gazing at the wind and seizing shadows.

Impatience

He plants a tree in the morning and wants to saw planks from it at evening.

The speed of the horseman must be limited by the speed of his horse.

If you are not patient in small things, you will bring great plans to nought.

Imprudence

Never insult an alligator until you have crossed the river.

He has both feet planted firmly in the air.

He who takes the raven for a guide will be led to the carcasses of dogs.

A person who sees advantages but not disadvantages is like a fish that sees only the bait but not the hook.

Do not quench your thirst with poisoned wine.

Do not seek to escape from a flood by clinging to a tiger's tail.

It is not evidence of strength in a man to throw himself into an abyss.

Indifference

As he is not personally involved, what he says belongs to the category of 'cool wind'.

This is but an eddy on the surface of a moving stream. It comes and it goes, and the waters press on as before.

In-Fighting

Be sure you have the support of your equals before you challenge your superiors.

No one can have a higher opinion of him than I have—and I think that he is a dirty little beast.

I would like to treat him like a treasure—bury him in the ground with loving care.

Breathe on the surface of his self-repose as a summer breeze moves on the smooth water of a mountain lake—not deeply but never quite at rest.

Inflexibility

There is no sadder or more frequent obituary on the pages of time than 'we have always done it this way'.

The defects are almost always more tolerable than the change necessary for their removal.

To chisel the foot to suit the shoe.

Ingratitude

To break the bridge by which one has crossed.

When he was a puppy, I brought him up.
When he became a dog, he bit me.

When a tree falls, the monkeys disperse.

When you drink the water, remember the spring.

Insincerity

The cat weeping over the rat.

Lips assenting, heart dissenting.

Insufficiency

A crumb in an empty bread box.

He has only a solitary spear and a single horse.

He tries to make waves without wind.

A single tree cannot make a forest.

You can't clap with one hand.

Intelligence

You need luck to inherit brains.

Many complain of their looks, but no one complains of his brains.

He is mediocre—not close to wise and not far from foolish.

You say one thing, he understands three things.

Job Suitability

If a man lives near the hills, he must get his living from the hills; if near water, from the water.

Tigers don't eat grass!

The head of an ox cannot be fitted to the mouth of a horse.

I thought he was a young man of promise, but it appears he is a young man of promises.

Journalists

There is no way to bribe or twist,
Thank God, the British journalist,
But seeing what, unbribed, he'll do,
There simply is no reason to!

He says not a word of truth—even in prayer.

Judging People

How many poor are rich in mind, and how many rich are poor in mind.

The generality of princes, if they were stripped of their purple and cast naked into the world, would immediately sink to the lowest rank of society without a hope of emerging from their obscurity.

It may happen in a mean and base fellow to be a good fencer. The estimate and value of a man consists in the heart and in the will.

It is not how much chaff is in you, but whether you have any wheat.

Even a bad coin must have two sides.

A gardener going into an orchard looks at the trees. He knows that this one is a date, that one a fig, the other a pomegranate, a pear, or an apple. To do this he does not have to see the fruit, only the trees.

Justice

A thousand deaths cannot atone for a grievous wrong.

Justice is the assurance that a law once made will not be broken in favour of any individual. This implies nothing about the ethical value of any such law.

Everything has two ends and a middle. The middle agrees most with justice.

Difficulty in obtaining justice Heaven is high above, and the Emperor is far away.

Kindness

Kindness is a language that the deaf can hear and the blind can read.

To refuse in a kind manner is better than to make long promises.

Labour

Nothing can move the man who is paid by the hour. How sweet the flight of time seems to his calm mind.

The man on horseback knows nothing of the toil of the traveller on foot.

No labour, however humble, dishonours a man.

Work expands to fill the time available for it.

My father taught me to work, he did not teach me to love it.

'Does the road wind uphill all the way?'
'Yes, to the very end.'
'Will the day's journey take the whole long day?'
'From morn to night my friend.'

Every work finds its man.

Law and Lawyers

A state is best governed when, with few laws, these are rigidly administered.

A lean compromise is better than a fat lawsuit.

That which is for the lawyer he writes down and what is against him he strikes out.

I was never ruined but twice: once when I lost a lawsuit, and once when I won one.

Maintain the law as a mountain.

Lawyers are the only persons in whom ignorance of the law is not punished.

When you have no basis for an argument, abuse the plaintiff.

Lawyer's Ethic When in trouble tell the truth; if still in trouble, tell the whole truth.

Laziness

A neglected talent is like a pearl lost in the sea.

Half-ploughed ground always means a poor yield.

Weakness married laziness, and their progeny was poverty.

That which is put off from today is put off from tomorrow.

The less one has to do, the less time one finds to do it in.

Laziness travels so slowly that poverty soon overtakes him.

To learn to be industrious takes three years; to learn to be lazy takes only three days.

Here he comes, at a snail's trot.

Leadership

To raise an army of ten thousand is easy, but where, oh where, to find a general?

Before you can lead, you must learn to follow.

In times of confusion, every active genius finds the place assigned to him by nature.

In human life, the most important scenes will depend on the character of a single actor.

To be a leader of men one must turn one's back on men.

To take the initiative is to gain the upper hand.

Liars

Nine out of ten matchmakers are liars.

Do not trust him who lies for thee, for he is as ready to lie against thee.

A half truth is a whole lie.

The clever liar gives no details.

Life

To have thoroughly tasted the sweet and the bitter.

A man's life is like a sunbeam passing through a crevice.

Life is unfair.

So long as you float on the deep ocean of the world, its waves will receive and repel you, turn by turn.

Come, for Hope's strong castle is built on weak foundations; bring wine, for the fabric of life is as unstable as the wind.

Life is not a matter of holding good cards, but of playing a poor hand well.

A man's life does not fill a hundred years, but always is it full of a thousand years' cares.

The years pass unperceived, and all changes but the heart of man.

My days are swifter than a weaver's shuttle.

Life is passing. This isn't a rehearsal, this is the main event!

Rejoice at your life, for the time is more advanced than you would think.

The wise man lives as long as he ought, not as long as he can.

The intoxication of youth is stronger than the intoxication of wine.

Then let us love one another and laugh. Time passes, and we shall soon laugh no longer—and meanwhile common living is a burden, and earnest men are at siege upon us all around.

Love

When you can explain love, you will have killed it.

Love takes no advice.

Love is sweet, but better with bread.

Love which never reproves is not love.

Love makes us blind, deaf and dumb.

Love me a little less, but longer.

Luck

The fox favoured by fortune, conquers the lion favoured by strength.

Take care to associate with him on whom fortune smiles.

Luck has a habit of visiting the industrious, the vigilant and the brave.

Management

Treat thy subordinate with kindness, thy equal with justice and thy superior with prudence.

The poor manager costs much more than the good manager.

Let the other man do his job without your interference.

You cannot teach management but you can teach things which are useful to managers.

When brains are needed, muscles won't help.

One of the most important managerial qualities is courage.

Meanness

If you insist on buying poor food, you must be prepared to dislike it at the serving.

Monday's funeral baked meats do service for Tuesday's wedding.

A lean dog shames his master.

Memory

I have a grand memory for forgetting.

The human memory is a very faulty piece of machinery, which requires a great deal of servicing.

Mistakes

The error of the learned is like a wrecked ship; it sinks and many are lost with it.

An error of an inch ends up a thousand miles off the mark.

Mankind only settles into the right course after passing through and exhausting all the varieties of error.

Business misjudgements and wrong turns are like tuberculosis; hard to detect and easy to cure in the beginning, and easy to detect and very hard to cure at the end.

Those who cannot learn from the past are doomed to repeat it.

Mistakes are always made when people get to the easy places.

Money

With money a dragon, without money a worm.

Ten gold pieces will move the gods; a hundred will move heaven itself.

Money speaks sense in a language all nations understand.

A rich man's joke is always funny.

A golden hammer breaks an iron gate.

Money will open a blind man's eyes and will make a priest sell his prayer books.

Men think that they test money; money in reality tests men.

Money hides a thousand deformities.

If a little money does not go out, great money will not come in.

The rich add riches to riches; the poor add years to years.

There is more trouble in keeping money than in getting it.

Living in the lap of luxury isn't bad, except that you never know when luxury is going to stand up!

Sad is the man who has nothing but money.

Morale

Keep your broken arm inside your sleeve.

When you lose all your money, you have lost half, but when you lose courage you have lost all.

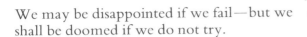

We may be disappointed if we fail—but we shall be doomed if we do not try.

Neighbours

It is certain that if a man hates at all, he will hate his neighbour.

Let thy foot be seldom in thy neighbour's house, lest he be weary of thee, and hate thee.

Obscurity

Like mountains seen through the clouds and mists.

In the dark, even the classics become obscure.

Old Age

Laugh at the old, and age will laugh at you.

The forties are the old age of youth, but the fifties are the youth of old age.

At seventy a man is a candle in the wind; at eighty, frost on the tiles.

The man who knows that deterioration is the rule of life won't take his troubles too seriously.

Old age is sickness enough.

For the ignorant, old age is winter; for the learned old age is the harvest.

If I knew I was going to live this long, I'd have taken better care of myself.

The day is ending, the way is long; my life already begins to stumble on its journey.

Opportunity

Seize opportunity by the forelock, for behind she is bald.

Where the ox clears a way, the sheep can surely follow.

A fly clinging to the tail of a swift horse.

Other Cultures

America is the country where you can buy a lifetime supply of aspirin for a dollar, and use it up in two weeks.

The difference between tragedy and comedy in German drama, is that the former features eight deaths and a suicide at a funeral, while the latter involves similar fatalities at a wedding.

Asia has a way of giving you just what it wants to give.

Parents

If you do not support your parents while alive, it is of no use to sacrifice to them when they are dead.

Good parents, happy marriages; good children, fine funerals!

Patience

The remedy for him who has no remedy, is patience.

There is necessarily a period between seed-time and harvest.

When fully ripe, the fruit falls of its own accord.

If you are patient in one moment of anger, you will escape a hundred days of sorrow.

Every beginning has an end.

However much the river winds, it finds the sea at last.

Patriotism

Were it not for patriotism, sterile lands would be deserted.

Beautiful or not, it is my native land. A relative or not, he is a fellow countryman.

The nobility of a land consists in its inhabitants, not in its soil.

Peace

There can be no real peace, only the absence of actual fighting.

If we open a quarrel between the past and the present, we shall find that we have lost the future.

Perseverance

Fall down seven times, get up eight.

Perseverance makes all things easy.

The compass points the way, but one's own laborious feet must make the journey.

Ninety miles is but half way in a journey of a hundred miles.

The mouse gets through an obstacle that a strong man cannot breach. It does so by ceaselessly nibbling at it.

There is marrow in this bone if you will but probe it.

Pity

These men know the pathos of life, and mortal things touch their hearts.

Don't drop a stone on a man who has fallen into a bear-pit.

Politics

An honest politician is one who when he is bought, will stay bought.

A man who is not a socialist in his youth has no heart, and a man who is not a capitalist in his maturity has no head.

Political language is designed to make lies sound truthful and murder respectable, and to give an appearance of solidity to pure wind.

When I was a boy I was told that anybody could become president. I am beginning to believe it.

Outdoor rustic people have not many ideas, but such as they have are hardy plants, and thrive flourishingly in persecution.

A bitter truth, rediscovered lately by many republicans, hailing their revolutionary leaders in the moment of independence, is that there is a permanent breed of men who love the bonfire but find the rebuilding something of a bore.

Poverty

I have tasted everything, and found nothing as bitter as begging.

Poverty comes from God, but not dirt.

It's no disgrace to be poor, but it's no honour either.

Industry breaks the chains of poverty.

He who lacks a single coin sees many bargains.

Power

You must steer the rudder according to the wind.

When the horse wags his tail, the flies disperse.

When the wind blows, the grass moves.

All power corrupts, but absolute power is absolutely delightful!

Pride

If your face is swollen with beating, pretend to be a fat man.

Even a hungry person will refuse food offered in contempt.

May the lion devour me, but not the dog.

Men's feelings are as thin as paper.

To bow the body is easy; to bow the will is hard.

Rather be a cock's beak than a bull's rump.

Even a frog thinks he has feathers.

Problems

As difficult as balancing an olive on a monk's head.

There are no one-dimensional problems.

Domestic appointments are not less troublesome for being less important.

To retrieve the past in the midst of a fierce and relentless present, is no easy matter.

Who can clear muddy water? If it keeps still, it clears of its own accord.

Every day brings its own troubles.

Bad figures take longer to add up than good ones.

Settle one difficulty and you keep a hundred others away.

Competing pressures tempt one to believe that an issue deferred is a problem avoided. More often it is a crisis invited.

Human institutions are trouble prone.

No obstacle is both too high to get over and too low to get under.

As the water subsides, so the rocks appear.

Seven–eighths of everything can't be seen.

Profit

Every blade of grass has a drop of dew.

If the profits are great, the risks are great.

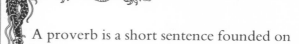

Promotion

When the water rises, the boat rises also.

To attach oneself to the tail of a swift horse.

Prospects

When the tree is full, the doubtful fruit remains on the branch.

Prospects—brilliant! Situation—desperate!

Proverbs

The proverb is to speech what salt is to food.

A proverb is a short sentence founded on long experience.

Proverbs are the precious distillation of what man has learned from centuries of experience.

Proverbs are the tears of humanity.

Prudence

Even a beggar will not cross a rotten wooden bridge.

In beating a dog, first find out who his owner is.

If travelling in the land of the one-eyed, cover one of thy eyes.

Light thy lamp before it gets dark.

Where the road bends abruptly, take short steps.

The hare does not eat the grass around his burrow.

Punishment

A little punishment—a great warning.

Beyond the reach of even a long whip.

The best way to avoid punishment is to fear it.

If one is to be hanged, it should be for a capital offence.

Rebukes

Never rebuke a man in such a way as to shame him in public.

Who loves thee scolds thee.

A rebuke entereth deeper into one that hath understanding, than a hundred stripes into a fool.

He that heareth reproof getteth understanding.

He who cannot accept reproof cannot become great.

Reciprocity

Even a goat and an ox must keep in step if they would plough together.

A man asked, 'Is there one word that will keep us on the path to the end of our days?' Yes, *reciprocity*. What you do not wish yourself, do not do to others.

One hand washes the other.

One family builds a wall, two families enjoy it.

What is lost in the morning is gained in the evening.

If you seek a brother to share your burden, brothers are hard to find. But if you are in search of someone whose own burden you will yourself share, there is no scarcity of such brothers.

Relatives

It is easy to govern a kingdom but difficult to rule one's family.

The seats in the great hall all come in rotation: the daughter-in-law will some day be the mother-in-law.

Even the Emperor has straw-sandalled relatives.

Do not transact business with him whom thou lovest for his love will soon come to an end.

Wife's relations Apron-string relatives.

Religion

What you are seeking in your retreat, I see clearly in every road and alleyway.

The monastery faces the convent; there is nothing going on—but there may be.

Reputation

If his word were a bridge, men would be afraid to cross it.

He is a worm-eaten cane.

One speck of rat's dung spoils a whole pot of rice.

In order to heighten your dignity, it is not necessary to stand upon it.

If you are standing upright, don't worry if your shadow is crooked.

In your town, your reputation counts; in another, your clothes do.

No office dignifies a man, but many a man dignifies his office.

Results

The shortest way to do many things, is to do only one thing at a time.

When the fruit is ripe, the time has come for the tree to be shaken.

To do much with feeble means is greater than to do more with large resources.

Rogues

A fox may grow grey, but never good.

A dagger hidden in a smile.

A league of foxes and a cabal of dogs.

His idea of a square deal is one in which he is protected on five sides.

He wipes tears off the opera mask.

Distrust a spider when it produces honey.

Distrust the threadbare person who from an upper backroom invites you to join him in an infallible process of enrichment.

Rumour

Of three words that reach our ears, two will be evil.

A word whispered in the ear can carry a thousand miles.

A falling body always rolls to the most inaccessible spot.

Things are always in the very last place we search—for who searches after finding?

Self-Interest

When times are easy we do not burn incense, but when trouble comes we embrace the feet of the Buddha.

It is the politest pig that loses his place at the trough.

If you angle with a straight hook, only those fish which are willing, get on it.

Searching

The easiest way to find something lost around the house is to buy a replacement.

Other men's misfortunes are not hard to bear.

What is worth doing, is worth doing for the money.

Do not burn down your house in order to inconvenience even your mother-in-law.

Sex

The thing that takes up the least amount of time and causes the most amount of trouble, is sex.

Office entanglements Never get your meat from the same place that you get your bread.

Shame

To shame a man in public is like shedding his blood.

Shame fades in the morning, debts remain from day to day.

Do not sit down in a place where they might command thee, 'Get up'.

Silence

Silence is the brother of assent.

There is nothing so deep as the unspoken.

I have never regretted my silence, but often regretted my speech.

The greatest revelation is stillness.

Sin

There is no door to hell, but many choose to bore a hole to get in.

O Lord, give me chastity and self restraint— but do not give it yet!

Sincerity

Rock stands, and mud washes away.

Sincerity will compensate for a great deal of inadequacy.

Sorrow

One's heart is in ashes.

Alive he was honoured, dead he was lamented.

Not forever can one enjoy stillness and peace, but misfortune and destruction are not final. When the grass has been burnt by the fire of the steppe, it will grow anew in summer.

Speaking

To gnaw phrases and chew words.

A bachelor of arts discusses books; a pork butcher talks of pigs.

Conversation is an unrehearsed intellectual adventure in which the journey matters more than the destination.

Eloquence consists in making the speech comprehensible to the multitude and agreeable to the learned.

Words of gold and jade.

When Pericles spoke, the people said 'How well he orates'. When Demosthenes spoke, they cried 'Let us march'.

I cannot hear what you say, for the thunder of what you are.

Speculation

Nine chances to die and one to live.

Spring dreams.

To secure one, but lose ten thousand.

Spirit

A tiny spark of fire may set afire a whole prairie.

What the heart wills the hand obeys.

It harms a man far more to wound his spirit than to break his body.

His spirit was a very dead thing: withered, contentious, empty. A thistle in late autumn.

Statistics

Your statistics make no noise in my frying pan.

You can usually get all the figures, except those that you need.

Those directly concerned with data collection always strive for perfection. It takes a much wider responsibility to decide that the cost of perfection can be prohibitive.

Strength

Pray that you will never have to suffer all that you are able to endure.

Separate reeds are weak and easily broken, but bound together they are strong and hard to tear apart.

The army should always be ready, but never used.

Stubbornness

You can't make an ox bend his head if he doesn't want to drink.

In any change of policy or procedure, he can be relied upon to produce the improbable hypothetical situation in which the new policy cannot work.

There is no cure for stubbornness.

Subordinates

If the string is long the kite flies high.

Juniors are to be respected. How do we know that they will not be our equals in the future?

Success

Some vanquish by a single blow, others by efforts successfully repeated.

Every person has his own gold medal.

A great enterprise is unlikely to be achieved except at the sacrifice of everything else.

Suspicion

Respect the stranger—and remain suspicious.

One is the thief and many are the suspected.

If what we see before our eyes is doubtful, how can we believe all that is spoken behind our backs?

Sometimes we suspect the heart, even if the tongue be truthful.

Because two men lower their voice in the street, they are not necessarily planning a robbery.

In buying a needle, examine the eye.

Temptation

Don't put dry wood close to the fire.

There are terrible temptations which it requires strength and courage to yield to.

I can resist everything except temptation.

If you don't want anyone to know it, don't do it.

If girls were not pretty, men would completely ignore temptation.

Thinking

Don't ever get so busy that you haven't time to think.

Clear thinking, even if it leads to unwelcome conclusions, is better than muddled compromise or muted evasion.

There is no labour to which a man will not resort to avoid the real labour of thinking.

The cost is principally thought and hard work which, though often painful, are seldom fatal.

He thinks by infection, catching an opinion like a cold.

You may rob the three armies of their commander-in-chief, but you cannot deprive the humblest peasant of his opinion.

His thinking runs like sparks in a burnt-up paper—wherever the nutrition of the moment creates an opening, but nowhere else.

Time

A day seems as long as three autumns.

To one who waits, a moment seems like a year.

An inch of gold cannot buy an inch of time.

The East has all the time, the West has none.

Men of all sorts belong always to their own time.

Though the sea dries up and rocks decay.

The past is a foreign country. They do things differently there.

Tolerance

There is room on the road for everybody if each person will move a little to one side.

Leave a little of the tail to whisk off the flies.

He who smiles rather than rages is always the stronger.

The just man has a steady willingness to believe that his opponent is as honourable a man as himself, and may be right.

Keep your offence in your bosom and you may meet as before.

He who is not satisfied with the rule of Moses will have to be satisfied with the rule of Pharaoh.

Trading

Just scales and full measure injure no man.

The buyer has need of a hundred eyes, the seller of only one.

He who cannot smile, ought not to keep a shop.

Each trade has its own ways.

The attributes of a merchant are three hands and two faces.

To open a business is easy; the difficult thing is to keep it open.

Asking your competitor for help To ask the tiger if it could spare you its hide.

Buying cheaply is often buying dearly.

A melon seller never cries 'Bitter melons' nor a wine seller 'Thin wine'.

Those who sell dog-meat often display a lamb's head.

Eat in the dark the bargain that you purchased in the dusk.

Customers are the precious things. Goods are only grass.

No customer loyalty can survive a two per cent discount.

We do not run the business to serve the employees; nor do we run it to serve the shareholders. We run the business to serve our customers.

Travel

It is better to travel first class than to arrive.

A distant place The edge of the heaven and the corner of the sea.

A remote place South of the mountains and north of the seas.

Trust

The hand that feeds the ox, grasps the knife when it is fattened.

Trust everybody, but always cut the cards.

To be successful in business, integrity is vital. It may cost money in the short term. In the long term it is worth gold.

I trust you completely, but please send cash!

Truth

The worst libel can be the truth.

He who seeks the truth must listen to his opponent.

An example is not truth; it is only an example.

That which one sees can be believed. It is also said that that which one believes can be seen.

You may regret telling the truth.

Uselessness

To ask the way from a blind person.

He has acquired a stony field.

To try to pick up a needle in the sea.

As useful as sending a kiss by a messenger.

You are nailing a stick into an empty space.

Verbosity

If one word does not succeed then thousands are of no avail.

His reasons are as two grains of wheat hid in two bushels of chaff: you shall seek all day ere you find them, and when you have them, they are not worth the search.

Victory

Victory has many fathers—defeat is always an orphan.

Winning an argument does not necessarily convince the defeated opponent.

Visiting

Visiting is like rain; prayed for when absent, but tiresome when overdue.

It is easier to visit friends than to live with them.

Vulnerability

He who flies on an eagle's back must sooner or later drop off.

It is difficult to guard against hidden arrows.

He who thinks he is raising a mound may in reality be digging a pit.

There are times when even the tiger sleeps.

The great tree attracts the wind.

A swallow's nest on a tent.

Although we may protect the fruit, we cannot see the roots.

Weakness

A sheep's body in a tiger's skin.

Every fence has a rotten stake somewhere.

Eggs must not quarrel with stones.

Too weak to bear the weight of clothes.

Last night I had many resolutions, but this morning I went my old way.

From bad to worse is an easy step.

Advance an inch and retreat a foot.

The wind sweeps away stray clouds.

Wisdom

A wise man leaves little to chance.

Of wisdom, half comes with birth, half comes with learning.

The wise man can adapt himself to circumstances as water takes the shape of the gourd that holds it.

As a solid rock is not shaken by the wind, wise people waver not amidst blame and praise. Wise people become serene.

Grey hair is a sign of age, not wisdom.

True wisdom consists in knowing your own capacity and stopping at once when something is too much for you.

The wise know, because they have paid for their wisdom. You do not accept their counsel because it is offered for so much less than they have paid for it.

Wives

A shrewish wife can, alas, be right.

Curse not your wife in the evening, or you will have to sleep alone.

Taking a wife is like buying nuts; one has to go largely by the outside.

A man without a wife is a homeless wanderer.

It does no harm to listen to one's wife.

The man who marries for money, earns it.

There is a substitute for everything except the wife of one's youth.

Worry

Men are tormented with the opinions they have of things and not by the things themselves.

That the birds of worry and care fly above your head, this you cannot change; but that they build nests in your hair, this you can prevent.

The greatest of worries cannot pay the smallest of debts.

When things do not get better, don't worry—they may get worse!

Zeal

The current of zeal and devotion, if contracted into a narrow channel, runs with the strength, and sometimes the fury, of a torrent.

Single-mindedness, whether the aim is lofty or selfish, has the power to achieve its ends.